DISCOVERING DINOSAURS
MIGHTY GIANTS

INTERNET LINKED

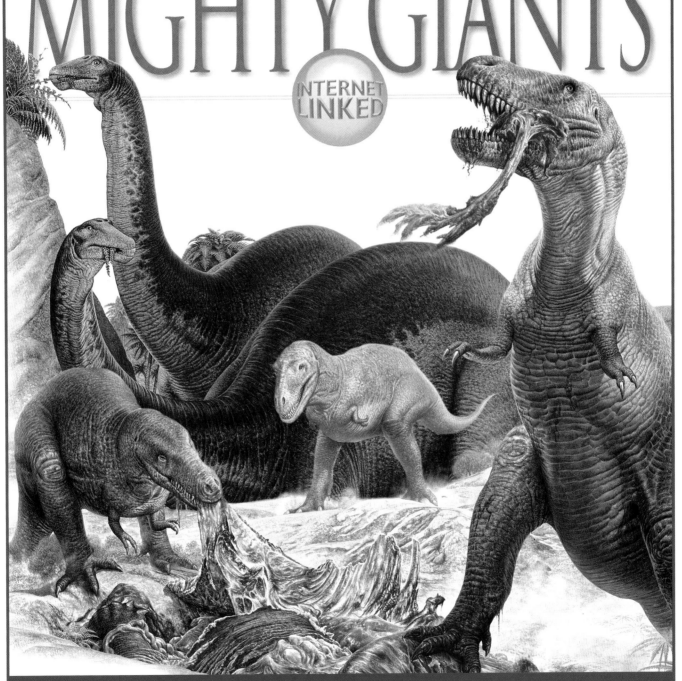

MICHAEL BENTON

GREENWICH EDITIONS

INTERNET SAFETY

Always follow these guidelines for a fun and safe
journey through cyberspace:

1. Ask your parents for permission before you go online.

2. Spend time with your parents online
and show them your favourite sites.

3. Post your family's e-mail address, even if you have your own
(only give your personal address to someone you trust).

4. Do not reply to e-mails if you feel
they are strange or upsetting.

5. Do not use your real surname while you are online.

6. Never arrange to meet 'cyber friends' in person
without your parents' permission.

7. Never give out your password.

8. Never give out your home address or telephone number.

9. Do not send scanned pictures of yourself
unless your parents approve.

10. Leave a website straight away if you find something that is
offensive or upsetting. Talk to your parents about it.

This edition published in 2005 by Greenwich Editions
The Chrysalis Building, Bramley Road, London W10 6SP

© 2002 Zigzag Children's Books

An imprint of **Chrysalis** Books Group

Author: Professor Michael Benton
Consultant: Dougal Dixon BSc (Hons), MSc
Illustrator: John Sibbick
Digital Retouch Artist: Steve Sweet

Editorial Director: Honor Head
Art Director: Simon Rosenheim
Senior Editor: Rasha Elsaeed
Project Editor: Jane Yorke
Assistant Editor: Clare Chambers
Project Designer: Sarah Crouch
Assistant Designers: Keren-Orr Greenfeld, Zeta Jones

ISBN 0-86288-709-7

British Library Cataloguing in Publication Data for this book is available from the British Library

Printed and bound in China

CONTENTS

Earth's Largest Beasts   4
Giant Reptiles Up Close   6

Monster Predators: Theropods
Terrifying T. Rex   8
Tyrant Hunters   10
Jurassic Killers   12
Theropods Up Close   14

Peaceful Giants: Prosauropods and Sauropods
The First Plant-eaters   16
Classic Giants   18
The Biggest Ever?   20
Body Defences   22
Sauropods Up Close   24

Bird-footed Runners: Ornithopods
Two-legged Monsters   26
The Duckbills   28
Ornithopods Up Close   30

Index   32

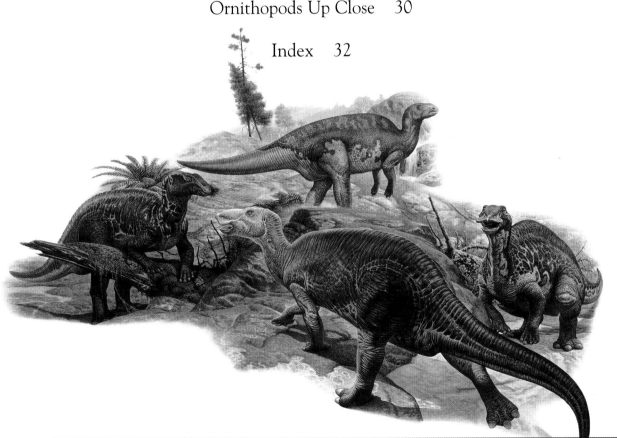

EARTH'S LARGEST BEASTS

Dinosaurs are famous for being big. The biggest, such as *Brachiosaurus* or *Diplodocus*, were ten times the size of an elephant – the biggest land animal today.

The largest complete skeleton found is of *Brachiosaurus*. It measured 22 metres long and 12 metres tall – about as high as a tall tree. Bones found in the United States show that there may have been dinosaurs called *Supersaurus* and *Ultrasaurus*. These creatures would have been a third larger than *Brachiosaurus*, making them the biggest animals ever to have lived on Earth. By contrast, the smallest dinosaurs were about the same size as a chicken.

All dinosaurs belonged to a group of animals called reptiles. Reptiles have a backbone and scaly, waterproof skin. Most of them lay eggs. Today, reptiles include lizards, snakes, tortoises and crocodiles. Unlike crocodiles, which have short, sprawling legs and live in water, dinosaurs walked on upright, thick legs and lived on land.

No one has ever seen a living dinosaur. Scientists call the dinosaur age the Mesozoic Era. Different dinosaurs lived at different times. The biggest dinosaurs appeared around 200 to 150 million years ago.

Muttaburrasaurus

Camptosaurus

Iguanodon

HOW DO I SAY THAT?

MESOZOIC
MESS-OH-ZOH-IK

CRETACEOUS
KRET-AY-SHUSS

JURASSIC
JOO-RASS-IK

TRIASSIC
TRY-ASS-IK

Theropods

A group of dinosaurs that included all huge, two-legged meat-eaters. Allosaurus had razor-sharp teeth. Ceratosaurus is famous for the unusual 'horns' on its face.

Ouranosaurus

Ceratosaurus

Ornithopods

These were plant-eaters. While not the biggest dinosaurs, the largest ornithopods were known for their big heads, horse-like snouts, strong hind legs and broad feet that supported their bulk. The four iguanodontids here had flat, hoof-like claws, making them more suited to walking than grasping objects.

Allosaurus

Sauropods

Plant-eating dinosaurs sauropods had gigantic barrel-shaped bodies, pillar-like legs and massive feet. They include Apatosaurus *and* Diplodocus.

Apatosaurus

FACTFILE: THE DINOSAUR AGE

- The Mesozoic Era lasted from 250 to 65 million years ago. Mesozoic means 'middle life'.

- The Cretaceous Period lasted from 150 to 65 million years ago. Cretaceous comes from the Latin *creta* ('chalk').

- The Jurassic Period lasted from 200 to 150 million years ago. It was named after the Jura Mountains, France.

- The Triassic Period lasted from 250 to 200 million years ago. Triassic means 'three-part'.

5

GIANT REPTILES

Why were some dinosaurs so big? Large animals have a lot of advantages. A big carnivore can kill almost anything, so it will never go hungry. A huge herbivore can be so big that no meat-eater can attack it – think of a lion trying to eat an elephant. Big animals can cover long distances in search of food. However, large animals have to eat a lot. Their weight can put a strain on their bones, causing health problems such as arthritis.

The longest dinosaur known was *Diplodocus*. Its skeleton measured 27 metres in length. Giants like *Diplodocus* weighed about 50 tonnes. It had four legs, so each leg had to support more than 10 tonnes. Its backbone was like the flat roadway of a bridge, slung between the hip girdle and the shoulder girdle. It needed strong muscles and ligaments just to support its huge weight. Giant dinosaurs could not move fast. If *Diplodocus* tried to gallop it would have broken its legs.

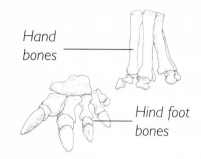

Hand bones

Hind foot bones

Big bones
Sauropods such as Brachiosaurus *had massive hands and feet to support their huge weight. The bones are enormous – each toe bone is as big as your thigh bone!*

Giant bridges
Sauropods are built like suspension bridges. A suspension bridge uses massive steel cables to hold up the flat road surface over which cars and people cross. In a sauropod, the backbone, long neck and tail, were held up by huge cable-like muscles and tendons that stretched along the back.

DINO DICTIONARY

- **Carnivore:** an animal that feeds on meat and flesh
- **Herbivore:** an animal that feeds on plants

Streamlined back
Sauropods had long spines on each vertebra. These spines held powerful muscles.

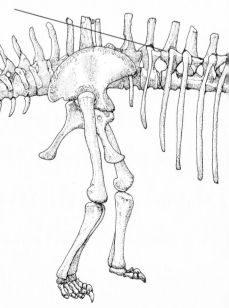

Tailing off
The sauropod tail was long and whip-like. It was made up of many very small vertebrae.

Strong tails
Spines above and below the tail vertebrae (segments of the backbone) helped the muscles whip the tail up and down and from side to side.

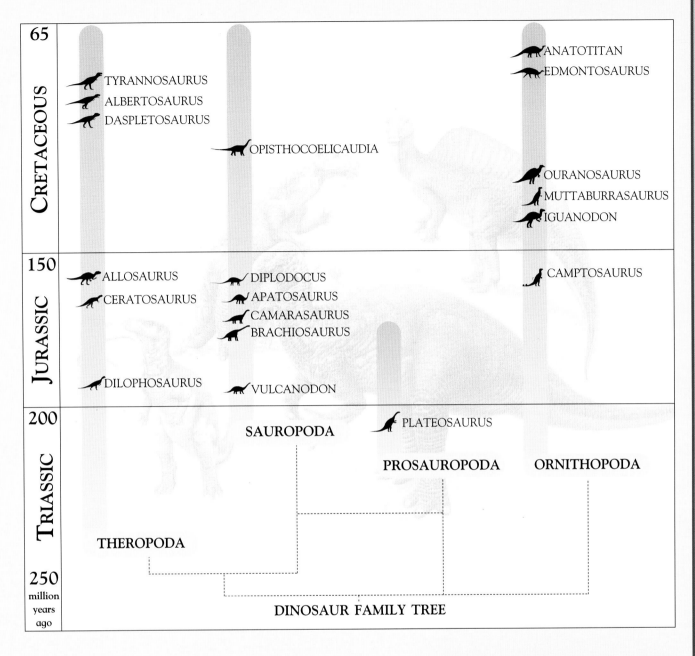

65			
CRETACEOUS	TYRANNOSAURUS ALBERTOSAURUS DASPLETOSAURUS	OPISTHOCOELICAUDIA	ANATOTITAN EDMONTOSAURUS OURANOSAURUS MUTTABURRASAURUS IGUANODON
150			
JURASSIC	ALLOSAURUS CERATOSAURUS DILOPHOSAURUS	DIPLODOCUS APATOSAURUS CAMARASAURUS BRACHIOSAURUS VULCANODON	CAMPTOSAURUS
200			
TRIASSIC	SAUROPODA PLATEOSAURUS PROSAUROPODA ORNITHOPODA THEROPODA		
250 million years ago	DINOSAUR FAMILY TREE		

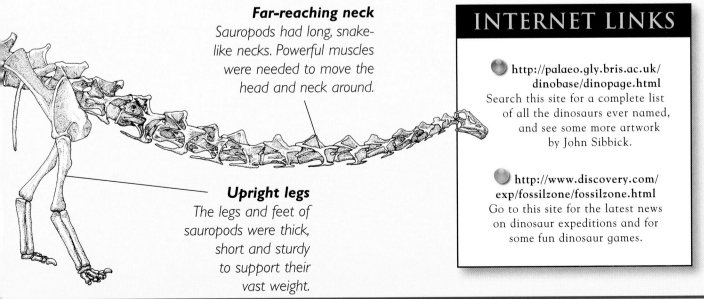

Far-reaching neck
Sauropods had long, snake-like necks. Powerful muscles were needed to move the head and neck around.

Upright legs
The legs and feet of sauropods were thick, short and sturdy to support their vast weight.

INTERNET LINKS

http://palaeo.gly.bris.ac.uk/
dinobase/dinopage.html
Search this site for a complete list
of all the dinosaurs ever named,
and see some more artwork
by John Sibbick.

http://www.discovery.com/
exp/fossilzone/fossilzone.html
Go to this site for the latest news
on dinosaur expeditions and for
some fun dinosaur games.

TERRIFYING T.REX

With a mouthful of razor-sharp teeth, each the size of a banana, *Tyrannosaurus rex* **is famous for being a fearsome predator.**

Was *Tyrannosaurus rex* a hunter that chased its prey at high speed, or was it a meat-eating scavenger? Fossil footprints give us clues about the speed and weight of a dinosaur. *T. rex* may have fed off slow-moving dinosaurs as well as dead animals. Some paleontologists (scientists who study fossils) believe that because *T. rex* was so heavy, it would not have been able to run much faster than you can. Fossil footprints made by *Tyrannosaurus* show that it could have outrun a rhinoceros, perhaps reaching 48 kilometres per hour. *T. rex* weighed as much as two elephants. This load would have put a lot of stress on its two leg bones. If the dinosaur tripped, it could never get up again.

Tail
When it ran, T. rex raised its tail high off the ground as a counter-balance.

Skull
T. rex had a huge head with deep, powerful jaws.

Feet
T. rex stood on two massive feet. It had a large claw at the end of each of its toes. A tiny fourth toe stuck out behind, but it did not reach the ground.

WHERE DID THEY LIVE?

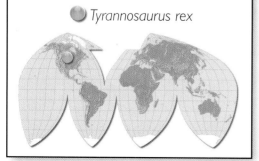

🔴 *Tyrannosaurus rex*

HOW DO I SAY THAT?

🔴 **TYRANNOSAURUS**
TIE-<u>RAN</u>-OH-<u>SAW</u>-RUS

Lived: 75 to 65 million years ago

Group: Theropoda

Size: 14 m long, 6 m tall

Weight: 6 to 7 tonnes

Discovery: 1902, Montana, USA

Diet: Carnivore

Special features: huge teeth, tiny arms

Name means: 'tyrant reptile'

Tyrannosaurus rex

Monster munch

Tyrannosaurus was twice as tall as an elephant and could have picked you up in its jaws. It fed by holding down prey with one foot and tearing the flesh into strips with its strong jaws. It is hard to see how T. rex used its tiny arms. They did not even reach its mouth!

9

TYRANT HUNTERS

Tyrannosaurids, such as *Albertosaurus* and *Daspletosaurus*, were relatives of *T. rex*. Being smaller, they moved much faster than most other theropods.

Like *T. rex*, *Albertosaurus* had only two fingers on its short arms. But *Albertosaurus* was probably more of an active hunter than *T. rex*. It would have killed its prey either by biting a lump of flesh from the neck, or by a powerful kick with its foot.

   Daspletosaurus lived at the same time as *Albertosaurus*. Scientists cannot explain how two different tyrannosaurids, were able to live without competing for the same food. *Daspletosaurus* had a heavier head and larger teeth than *Albertosaurus*, so perhaps it hunted different animals. Both were big enough to fight with faster dinosaurs, such as the duckbill hadrosaurs.

Powerful jaws
Daspletosaurus *may have killed its prey by snapping its jaws into the flanks of an animal, and leaving it to bleed to death.*

HOW DO I SAY THAT?

● **ALBERTOSAURUS**
AL-BERT-OH-SAW-RUS

● **DASPLETOSAURUS**
DASS-PLEET-OH-SAW-RUS

1. Daspletosaurus   2. Albertosaurus

Albertosaurus   Daspletosaurus

Moving in on the kill

Like many meat-eating animals today, Albertosaurus and other tyrannosaurids were probably attracted by the smell of blood and may have fought over a kill.

FACTFILE: ALBERTOSAURUS

Lived: 75 to 65 million years ago

Group: Theropoda

Size: 9 m long

Weight: 2 to 3 tonnes

Discovery: 1892, Alberta, Canada

Diet: Carnivore

Special features: powerful legs, tiny arms

Name means: 'Alberta reptile'

JURASSIC KILLERS

The first predators had huge heads, powerful jaws and ferocious teeth – which they used to sink into the flesh of other dinosaurs they hunted.

The dinosaur age is often linked to the word 'Jurassic'. This refers to the period of time when large, meat-eating theropods appeared – about 195 million years ago. The best-known Jurassic theropod was *Allosaurus.* Its powerful teeth could tear the flesh of its prey into large chunks. *Ceratosaurus* lived at the same time as *Allosaurus*, but it was half the size and fed on much smaller prey. *Ceratosaurus*, meaning 'horned reptile', had odd-looking bumps on its skull that probably made it look more frightening. *Dilophosaurus* lived earlier in the Jurassic Period. It is famous for a pair of crests on top of its head. The crests looked like two halves of a dinner plate set up on end.

1. Ceratosaurus 2. Dilophosaurus
3. Allosaurus

Dilophosaurus

Ceratosaurus

HOW DO I SAY THAT?

⬤ **ALLOSAURUS**
AL-OH-SAW-RUS

◗ **CERATOSAURUS**
SEE-RAT-OH-SAW-RUS

◖ **DILOPHOSAURUS**
DIE-LOW-FOE-SAW-RUS

WHERE DID THEY LIVE?

Allosaurus, Ceratosaurus and *Dilophosaurus*

FACTFILE: ALLOSAURUS

Lived: 160 to 150 million years ago

Group: Theropoda

Size: 12 m long

Weight: 4 to 5 tonnes

Discovery: 1877, Colorado, USA

Diet: Carnivore

Special features: massive skull, powerful hands

Name means: 'other reptile'

Fossil find

When 5000 *Allosaurus* bones were found in a quarry in Utah, USA, this large meat-eater became the best-known Jurassic theropod. It had sharp teeth and strong hands, each with three clawed fingers. It killed its prey by clamping its jaws around the animal's neck.

Allosaurus

13

THEROPODS

The first theropods had long arms and strong hands, with five fingers. They may have used the fingers seize and hold down its prey. Dinosaurs that came later, such as *Tyrannosaurus*, had short arms with two fingers, and short, strong thigh bones. This means that these later theropods may have been good runners. Theropods had blade-like, jagged teeth that curved into the mouth. Once the theropod sunk its jaws into its victim's flesh, the prey could not escape.

Theropods may have hunted in packs. Big predators, such as *Tyrannosaurus* and *Allosaurus,* probably hunted alone. They chased their prey, wrestling it to the ground and killed it by biting its neck. This is how lions and tigers hunt today. Large theropods probably hunted by stealth – staying very still until a plant-eater came near or creeping slowly through the trees and bushes until they were within striking distance. Then, with a quick leap, they would capture their prey!

Run for your life!

T. rex had massive jaws and a powerful neck. This suggests that the dinosaur hunted by charging at its prey, such as this duckbill, and hitting it hard. Then T. rex would snap shut its enormous jaws around the animal's neck.

THE THEROPODS:

- *Albertosaurus*
- *Allosaurus*
- *Ceratosaurus*
- *Daspletosaurus*
- *Dilophosaurus*
- *Tyrannosaurus*

INTERNET LINKS

http://www.ucmp.berkeley.edu/diapsids/saurischia/theropoda.html
Find out about the main groups of theropods.

http://www.newscientist.com/hottopics
Click on 'Dinosaurs' and get the latest news about *T. rex* and other species.

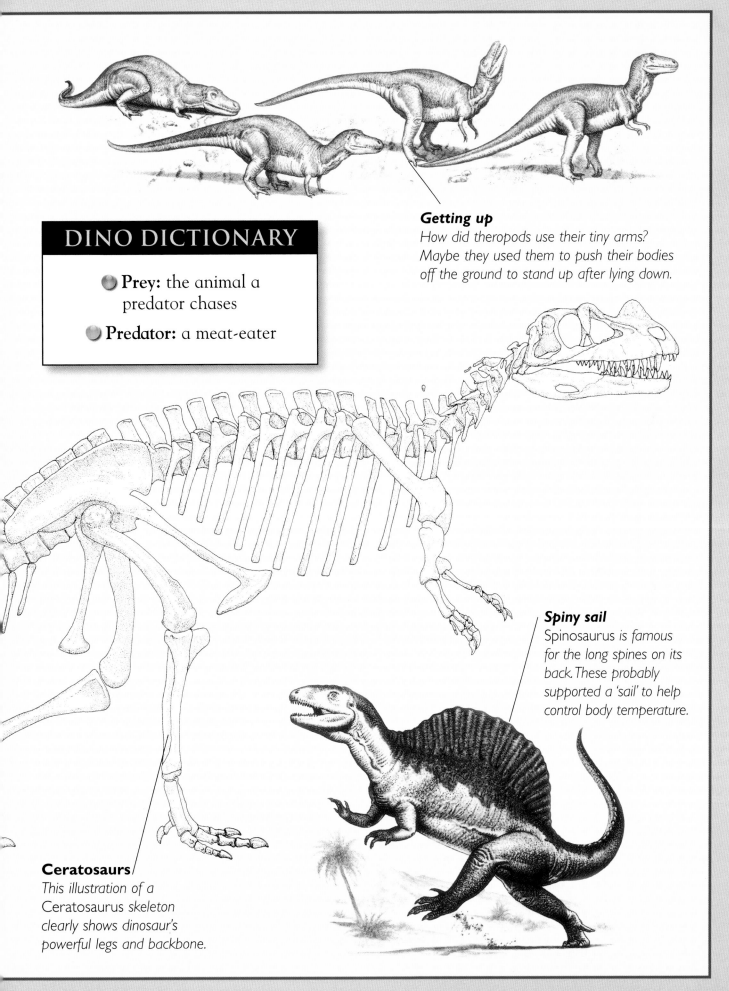

DINO DICTIONARY

⬤ **Prey:** the animal a predator chases

⬤ **Predator:** a meat-eater

Getting up
How did theropods use their tiny arms?
Maybe they used them to push their bodies
off the ground to stand up after lying down.

Spiny sail
Spinosaurus *is famous
for the long spines on its
back. These probably
supported a 'sail' to help
control body temperature.*

Ceratosaurs
*This illustration of a
Ceratosaurus skeleton
clearly shows dinosaur's
powerful legs and backbone.*

15

THE FIRST PLANT-EATERS

The true giants of the dinosaur age – the sauropods – evolved from medium-sized prosauropods such as *Plateosaurus*.

The first dinosaurs were human-sized, meat-eating reptiles. They appeared in the middle of the Triassic Period, around 230 million years ago. Then came the bigger, plant-eating 'early sauropods', known as the prosauropods. Later, prosauropods evolved (developed over a long time) into the gigantic sauropods, such as *Diplodocus* and *Apatosaurus,* of the Jurassic Period.

The first large prosauropod was *Plateosaurus.* This dinosaur was eight metres long. It was the largest land animal that had ever existed. Like all prosauropods, *Plateosaurus* walked on four legs, but it was light enough to stand easily or run on two legs. When standing, *Plateosaurus* used its huge hands, armed with claws, to pull tree branches to its mouth. Other large prosauropods included *Massospondylus* in South America and *Lufengosaurus* in Asia. Sauropods were heavier and four-footed. They were similar to *Plateosaurus* with their long, slender bodies, whip-like tails, enormously long necks and thin, pencil-shaped teeth.

HOW DO I SAY THAT?

● PLATEOSAURUS
<u>PLAT</u>-EE-OH-<u>SAW</u>-RUS

Armed and dangerous!
Plateosaurus *had huge, powerful hands armed with long claws. The thumb was very strong and carried the largest claw.*

Plateosaurus

FACTFILE: PLATEOSAURUS

- Lived: 220 to 205 million years ago
- Group: Prosauropoda
- Size: 6 to 8 m long
- Weight: 4 to 6 tonnes
- Discovery: 1837, Germany
- Diet: Herbivore
- Special features: powerful hands, walks on two or four legs
- Name means: 'flat reptile'

Hands up!
As a plant-eater, Plateosaurus *needed special hands that could support its weight, grasp tree branches and fight off predators.*

WHERE DID THEY LIVE?

Plateosaurus   Other prosauropods

Quick getaway
Plateosaurus *fed close to the ground or high up in the trees. It moved around on all fours. When alarmed, it would rear up and run away on its hind legs.*

CLASSIC GIANTS

The biggest dinosaurs of all time were the sauropods. *Diplodocus* **and** *Apatosaurus* **were the best known, with their long, snake-like necks.**

Diplodocus is the longest sauropod that ever existed, measuring 27 metres from snout to tail. Why did sauropods have such long necks? It was probably to help them feed with less effort. Instead of wandering about, *Diplodocus* stood still and swept its head from side to side over a wide area of plants. When you weigh 30 tonnes, this takes much less energy than moving around all the time.

When fossils of *Apatosaurus* bones were first found, the skeleton had no head. It was suspected that the creature was the short-snouted *Camarasaurus*. Later study showed that it was *Apatosaurus* – a close relative of *Diplodocus* with a much longer head.

On the receiving end
Some scientists believe that the sauropods used their enormously long tails to hit their enemies.

HOW DO I SAY THAT?

⬤ **APATOSAURUS**
AH-PAT-OH-SAW-RUS
⬤ **DIPLODOCUS**
DIP-LOD-O-KUS

1. Apatosaurus 2. Diplodocus

FACTFILE: APATOSAURUS

- Lived: 160 to 150 million years ago
- Group: Sauropoda
- Size: 21 m long
- Weight: 30 tonnes
- Discovery: 1877, Colorado, USA
- Diet: Herbivore
- Special features: long neck, heavy body
- Name means: 'deceptive reptile'

Vegetarian life

Plant-eating dinosaurs had to eat a lot to stay healthy. Grass did not appear on Earth until after the dinosaurs had become extinct. Apatosaurus might have fed on tough plants called ferns. It stripped the leaves off with its blunt, pencil-like teeth. Apatosaurus probably had stones inside its stomach to help grind up the plants.

WHERE DID THEY LIVE?

Apatosaurus and *Diplodocus*

THE BIGGEST EVER?

Most records of huge dinosaurs are based on limited fossil evidence – a giant leg bone or other parts of a monster skeleton. But few people doubt the enormity of *Brachiosaurus*.

Complete skeletons of *Brachiosaurus* were found in Tanzania, Africa, and they are huge. One of the skeletons is on display at the Humboldt Museum in Berlin, Germany, where it towers four floors high. With its long neck and enormous front legs, *Brachiosaurus* reached high above any other dinosaur to crop leaves from the tallest trees.

Camarasaurus was much smaller than *Brachiosaurus*. At 18 metres long, however, it was still the size of six elephants! The head of *Camarasaurus* had a short snout. The jaws were lined with sharp teeth to chew on tough vegetation. As with *Brachiosaurus* and all the giant, plant-eating dinosaurs, *Camarasaurus* had front legs that were shorter than the back legs. Its feet were heavily padded – to absorb the shock of impact from the creature's huge weight on the ground.

HOW DO I SAY THAT?

BRACHIOSAURUS
BRAK-EE-OH-SAW-RUS

CAMARASAURUS
KAM-AH-RA-SAW-RUS

Head first
Brachiosaurus *is the tallest known dinosaur. For such a mountain of flesh and bone, the head of this creature might seem strangely small.*

Sharp teeth
Herbivore Brachiosaurus had sharp, peg-like teeth for nibbling plants.

1. Camarasaurus 2. Brachiosaurus

FACTFILE: BRACHIOSAURUS

- Lived: 160-150 million years ago
- Group: Sauropoda
- Size: 22.5 m long, 12 m tall
- Weight: 50 tonnes
- Discovery: 1900, Colorado, USA
- Diet: Herbivore
- Special features: the tallest dinosaur, crest over eyes
- Name means: 'arm reptile'

WHERE DID THEY LIVE?

Brachiosaurus and Camarasaurus
Brachiosaurus

Short differences
Camarasaurus was *smaller than* Brachiosaurus. It had a shorter neck and front legs.

BODY DEFENCES

The sauropods were one of the longest-living family of dinosaurs. A range of body defences helped them to survive the predators of the Late Jurassic Period.

One of the first sauropods of the Early Jurassic was *Vulcanodon* from Zimbabwe, Africa. It was smaller than most sauropods, but at 6.5 metres long, it was big enough to have straight pillar-like legs to support its body. Most of the toes ended in short 'hooves', except for the thumb claw, which was long and sharp. Perhaps this claw was used as a form of defence to fight off predators.

By the end of the dinosaur age in the Late Cretaceous period, most of the sauropods were armoured with plates. These would have made it difficult for meat-eating dinosaurs to hunt them for food. *Saltasaurus,* from South America, had plates set in its skin. Large and small bony plates joined up to form a strong chain mail. *Opisthocoelicaudia,* from China, had an unusually strong tail. This helped the dinosaur prop itself on two legs. It may have also been used as a defending 'weapon'.

HOW DO I SAY THAT?

● OPISTHOCOELICAUDIA
OH-PISS-THO-SEE-LI-COW-DEE-AH
● SALTASAURUS
SAL-TA-SAW-RUS
● VULCANODON
VUL-KAY-NO-DON

Vulcanodon
Little is known about Vulcanodon, *because only one incomplete skeleton has been found. The name means 'volcano tooth' – the first fossil was found close to some ancient volcanic lavas.*

WHERE DID THEY LIVE?

- Opisthocoelicaudia
- Saltasaurus
- Vulcanodon

1. Opisthocoelicaudia 2. Saltasaurus 3. Vulcanodon

FACTFILE: SALTASAURUS

- Lived: 75 to 65 million years ago
- Group: Sauropoda
- Size: 12 m long
- Weight: 30 tonnes
- Discovery: 1980, Salta Province, Argentina
- Diet: Herbivore
- Special features: long neck, armour plates
- Name means: 'Salta reptile'

Tail props

Opisthocoelicaudia *had a strong, stiff tail. This dinosaur used its tail as a prop. It could reach high into the trees by rocking back on the tail and lifting its front quarters off the ground.*

Plate armour

Saltosaurus *is famous for its armour plates. This was probably a good defence against predators.*

23

SAUROPODS

When you look at a sauropod's skeleton, you can see that it is built for strength. The long neck and tail worked like the boom on a crane. In a large sauropod, the neck must have weighed about four tonnes, so it had to be strong. Powerful muscles and ligaments ran down the top of the neck. These could shorten to lift the neck up. The long whip-like tail could be raised and swung rapidly from side to side, probably to whack predators.

THE SAUROPODS:

- *Apatosaurus*
- *Brachiosaurus*
- *Camarasaurus*
- *Diplodocus*
- *Opisthocoelicaudia*
- *Plateosaurus*
- *Saltasaurus*
- *Vulcanodon*

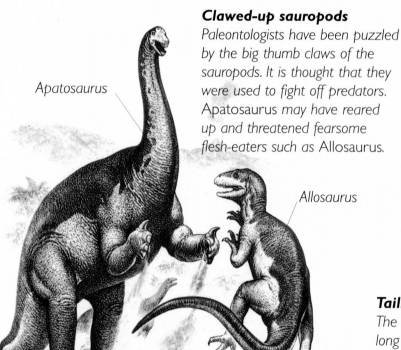

Clawed-up sauropods
Paleontologists have been puzzled by the big thumb claws of the sauropods. It is thought that they were used to fight off predators. Apatosaurus *may have reared up and threatened fearsome flesh-eaters such as* Allosaurus.

Apatosaurus

Allosaurus

Strong tails
Spines above and below the tail vertebrae helped the muscles whip the tail up and down and from side to side.

Tailing off
The sauropod tail was long and whip-like. It was made up of many very small vertebrae.

INTERNET LINKS

http://www.ucmp.berkeley.edu/diapsids/saurischia/sauropoda.html
Find out about all the groups of sauropod dinosaurs.

http://www.bbc.co.uk/dinosaurs/index.shtml
Find out about *Diplodocus* and all the other dinosaurs featured in the BBC's *Walking with Dinosaurs* programme.

DINO DICTIONARY

- **Paleontologist:** a scientist who studies fossils
- **Skeleton:** the bony framework that supports the body
- **Vertebra:** a small bone of the backbone

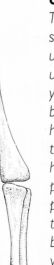

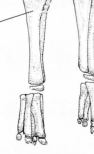

Wonder of the world

A complete skeleton of Brachiosaurus *has been put together from fossils collected in Africa around 1912. It can be seen in the Humboldt Museum in Berlin, Germany. The huge, powerful neck towers high into the exhibit hall, and people can walk under the dinosaur's belly.*

Streamlined back

Sauropods had long spines on each vertebra. These spines held powerful muscles.

Far-reaching neck

Sauropods had long, snake-like necks. Powerful muscles were needed to move the neck and head around.

Underwater swimmers?

This picture shows Brachiosaurus *standing in deep water. Scientists used to think that sauropods lived underwater. In the same way that your body floats in water, scientists believed that water would have helped support the huge weight of these dinosaurs. Sauropods could have floated in lakes and fed on plants around the lake edge. The problem with this theory is that these dinosaurs could not have breathed in deep water. Their lungs would have been about five metres below the surface. At that depth, the water pressure would have squashed their lungs.*

Sturdy legs

The legs and feet of sauropods were thick and short to support their vast weight.

25

TWO-LEGGED MONSTERS

These bird-footed runners attacked enemies with a vicious, dagger-like thumb claw.

The best-known ornithopod is *Iguanodon*. Its skeleton was one of the first ever to be found. *Iguanodon* stood and ran on its hind legs, but it could swing down on to its hands to feed on low-lying plants. *Iguanodon* had hooves on its feet and a mixture of hooves and claws on its hands.

The four ornithopods, shown together in this picture, lived in different parts of the world. *Iguanodon* is best known from fossil finds in Europe. *Ouranosaurus* lived in Africa and *Muttaburrasaurus* in Australia. *Camptosaurus*, an early ornithopod, came from North America.

HOW DO I SAY THAT?

● **CAMPTOSAURUS**
KAMP-TOE-<u>SAW</u>-RUS

● **IGUANODON**
IG-<u>WAN</u>-OH-<u>DON</u>

● **MUTTABURRASAURUS**
<u>MUT</u>-AH-<u>BUR</u>-AH-<u>SAW</u>-RUS

● **OURANOSAURUS**
OO-<u>RAN</u>-OH-<u>SAW</u>-RUS

Camptosaurus
An early ornithopod of the Late Jurassic.

1. Camptosaurus
2. Ouranosaurus
3. Muttaburrasaurus
4. Iguanodon

Ouranosaurus
Famous for the sail running along its back and tail.

Muttaburrasaurus
An ornithopod with a bump on its snout.

Defending claw
The large thumb claw of the ornithopods is a bit of a mystery. Why would a peaceful plant-eater have had such a lethal weapon? It may have been used to scare off enemies or to attract a mate.

Iguanodon
A dinosaur with huge, three-toed feet. Each toe ended with a small hoof instead of a claw.

WHERE DID THEY LIVE?

Camptosaurus   Iguanodon
Muttaburrasaurus   Ouranosaurus

THE DUCKBILLS

Recognised by their unusual heads, these fast-running, plant-eating ornithopods appeared late in the dinosaur age.

Hadrosaurs are also called 'duckbills' because of their duck-shaped heads. Duckbills were so similar that their skeletons are almost impossible to tell apart. The main differences are in the shape of the head. *Anatotitan* had a long, low snout. *Bactrosaurus* had a short snout, while *Kritosaurus* had a low hump in front of the eyes.

Duckbills lived mainly in North America and Asia in huge herds made up of different species. They relied on speed to escape from predators. Although they would go on all fours to feed, they rose up on their powerful back legs to run. Their tails stuck out behind as a counterbalance.

Balloon-face
Kritosaurus *had a low crest over its snout. This may have been covered with loose skin. It could then be blown up like a balloon when the creature bellowed.*

HOW DO I SAY THAT?

● **ANATOTITAN**
AH-<u>NAT</u>-OH-<u>TEE</u>-TAN

● **BACTROSAURUS**
<u>BAK</u>-TRO-<u>SAW</u>-RUS

● **EDMONTOSAURUS**
ED-<u>MONT</u>-OH-<u>SAW</u>-RUS

● **KRITOSAURUS**
<u>KRIT</u>-OH-SAW-<u>RUS</u>

FACTFILE: EDMONTOSAURUS

- Lived: 75 to 65 million years ago
- Group: Ornithopoda
- Size: 10 to 13 m long
- Weight: 8 to 10 tonnes
- Discovery: 1892, Alberta, Canada
- Diet: Herbivore
- Special features: duck-like snout, hooves on hand
- Name means: 'Edmonton reptile'

1. Bactrosaurus 2. Kritosaurus 3. Anatotitan 4. Edmontosaurus

Anatotitan and Edmontosaurus

Bactrosaurus   Kritosaurus

Bactrosaurus

This is one of the earliest hadrosaurs. It lived in Asia, so it would not have come across the three other North American dinosaurs.

Easy eating

Anatotitan shows its 'duckbill', which was used to gather plant food.

Edmontosaurus

One of the largest hadrosaurs, Edmontosaurus had hooved hands and feet, so that it could run on two or four legs.

29

ORNITHOPODS

Ornithopods had a mouthful of blunt teeth, which were perfect for grinding up plants. In fact, the duckbills had up to 300 teeth in each jaw, arranged in several rows. As the top row wore out the next row moved up to fill the gap.

Duckbills had large nostrils (the big openings at the front of the snout). This means that duckbills may have had a good sense of smell. They also may have been able to snort and bellow through their noses. The nose could have been used for signalling purposes, enabling the duckbill to produce distinctive calls. Some duckbills had such long noses, suggesting that they could have been used for feeding underwater. The nose could act as a snorkel so the creature could breathe while eating.

Hooves
Duckbills had small hooves on most of their fingers because the hands were used for walking.

Bellowing snouts
Duckbill hadrosaurs such as Edmontosaurus could bellow by inflating a balloon-like area of skin over their snouts.

THE ORNITHOPODS:

- *Anatotitan*
- *Bactrosaurus*
- *Camptosaurus*
- *Edmontosaurus*
- *Iguanodon*
- *Kritosaurus*
- *Maiasaura*
- *Muttaburrasaurus*
- *Ouranosaurus*

INTERNET LINKS

http://www.ucmp.berkeley.edu/diapsids/ornithischia/ornithopoda.html
Find out about all the ornithopod dinosaurs here.

http://www.zoomschool.com/subjects/dinosaurs/dinos/maiasaur.shtml
Find out more about *Maiasaura* – the 'good mother' dinosaur.

Back
Ornithopods often had little strips of criss-crossed bone along the backbone. These structures started out as flesh, but turned to bone to strengthen the back as the dinosaur grew older.

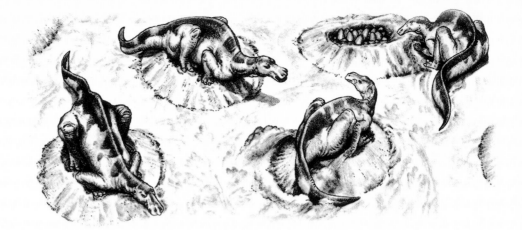

Parental care
Recent discoveries show that dinosaurs cared for their young. Maiasaura, a duckbill hadrosaur, is known as the 'good mother' dinosaur. Like all dinosaurs, it laid its eggs in shallow nests scooped out of the earth. Whole colonies of Maiasaura nests have been found, and there is evidence that the mothers laid their eggs, covered them, and then guarded the nests. Each female dinosaur in the colony would look after her eggs, keeping her distance from her neighbours. When the eggs hatched, the parents brought them soft plants to eat. This parental care continued until the young grew old enough to look after themselves.

Tail
Long, rib-like bones ran underneath the tail. These indicate that the ornithopods had powerful muscles in their tails.

Legs
Ornithopods had strong, pillar-like legs, which were designed for support and long spells of running. They needed these powerful legs so that they outrun their predators.

DINO DICTIONARY

● **Parental care:** the mother and father look after the young

INDEX

A

Albertosaurus 10–11
Allosaurus 5, 12, 13, 14, 24
Anatotitan 28, 29
Apatosaurus 5, 18–19, 24
armour 22, 23

B

Bactrosaurus 28, 29
bellowing 28, 30
bones 6
Brachiosaurus 4, 6, 20–21, 25
bridges 6

C

Camarasaurus 20, 21
Camptosaurus 4, 26, 27
carnivores (meat-eaters) 6, 8–15
ceratosaurs 15
Ceratosaurus 5, 12, 13
crests, head 12
Cretaceous Period 5, 7

D

Daspletosaurus 10–11
Dilophosaurus 12, 13
Diplodocus 5, 6, 18, 19
'duckbills' 28–29

E

Edmontosaurus 28, 29, 30
eggs 31

F

family tree 7
footprints, *T. rex* 8

H

hadrosaurs 28–29, 30
herbivores (plant-eaters) 6, 16–31
herds 28
Humboldt Museum 20, 25

I

Iguanodon 26, 27
iguanodontids 5
Internet links 7, 14, 24, 30

J

Jurassic Period 5, 7
  meat-eating theropods 12–13

K

Kritosaurus 28, 29

L

Lufengosaurus 16

M

Maiasaura 31
Massospondylus 16
meat-eaters 6, 8–15
Mesozoic Era 4, 5
Muttaburrasaurus 4, 26, 27

N

nests 31
nose, of hadrosaurs 30

O

Opisthocoelicaudia 22, 23
ornithopods 5, 7, 26–31
Ouranosaurus 5, 26, 27

P

paleontologists 25
parental care 31
plant-eaters 6, 16–31
Plateosaurus 16–17
predators 15
prey 15
prosauropods 7, 16–17

R

reptiles 4

S

'sails' 15, 27
Saltasaurus 22, 23
sauropods 5, 7, 18–25
  skeleton 6–7
size 4–5, 20
skeleton
  ornithopod 30–31
  sauropod 6–7, 24–25
  theropod 8, 14–15
snout, of duckbills 30
Spinosaurus 15
stomach, stones in 19
Supersaurus 4

T

tail
  of ornithopods 28, 31
  of sauropods 6, 18, 22, 23, 24
teeth
  of duckbills 30
  of theropods 14
temperature, body 15
theropods 5, 7, 8–15
thumb claws
  of ornithopods 27
  of sauropods 22, 24
Triassic Period 5, 7
tyrannosaurids 10–11
Tyrannosaurus rex 8–9, 14

U

Ultrasaurus 4

V

vertebrae 25
Vulcanodon 22, 23

W

water, living or feeding in 25, 30

Y

young, dinosaur 31

ANIMALS OF THE NIGHT

Design
David West
Children's Book Design
Illustrations
Stella Robinson
Picture Research
Cecilia Weston-Baker
Editor
Scott Steedman
Consultant
Miles Barton

© Aladdin Books Ltd 1989

Designed and produced by
Aladdin Books Ltd
70 Old Compton Street
London W1

First published in
Great Britain in 1989 by
Franklin Watts
12a Golden Square
London W1

ISBN 0 86313 975 2

Printed in Belgium

This book tells you about animals that are
active at night – where they live, what they eat
and how they survive. Find out some surprising
facts about them in the boxes on each page.
The identification chart at the back of the book
will help you when you see night creatures in
zoos or in the wild.

The little squares show
you how big the animal
is, compared to a
person.

A red square means that
the animal is endangered
in part or all of its range.
See the survival file.

The picture opposite shows a Bushbaby, an African night animal

FIRST SIGHT

ANIMALS OF THE
NIGHT

Lionel Bender

GLOUCESTER PRESS
London · New York · Toronto · Sydney

Introduction

As night falls many animals, including people, go to sleep or to rest in their homes. But other animals are just beginning their survival routines. These animals of the night are said to be "nocturnal". By being active during the hours of darkness, they make use of food sources and habitats that are used by other animals when the sun is out. They are also safe from predators that hunt during the day.

Most nocturnal creatures are highly adapted to life with little or no light. They can find their way, locate food and detect dangers in almost total darkness.

Contents

Special senses **6**
Aerial hunters **8**
Scavengers and predators **10**
Bats **12**
Avoiding the heat **14**
Spiders and scorpions **16**
Primates **18**
Urban visitors **20**
Frogs and toads **22**
Insect-eaters **24**
Pouched animals **26**
Survival file **28**
Identification chart **30**
Make a night-time animal mural **30**
Index **32**

◁ **Fennec Foxes do most of their exploring at night**

Special senses

Nocturnal animals have at least one sense – sight, hearing, smell, taste or touch – which is highly developed. These powerful senses help them to survive in the dark. Tigers, for example, have excellent eyesight and hearing and a keen sense of smell. Their eyes face forward, allowing them to judge distances accurately when they hunt at night.

Rattlesnakes and pythons can locate their prey in total darkness. They do this by using the heat-sensitive pits on their jaws. The pits help them detect small animals, such as rats and birds, which are warmer than their surroundings. These heat sensors can tell temperature differences of only one-thousandth of a degree Celsius.

Male moth with large, sensitive antennae

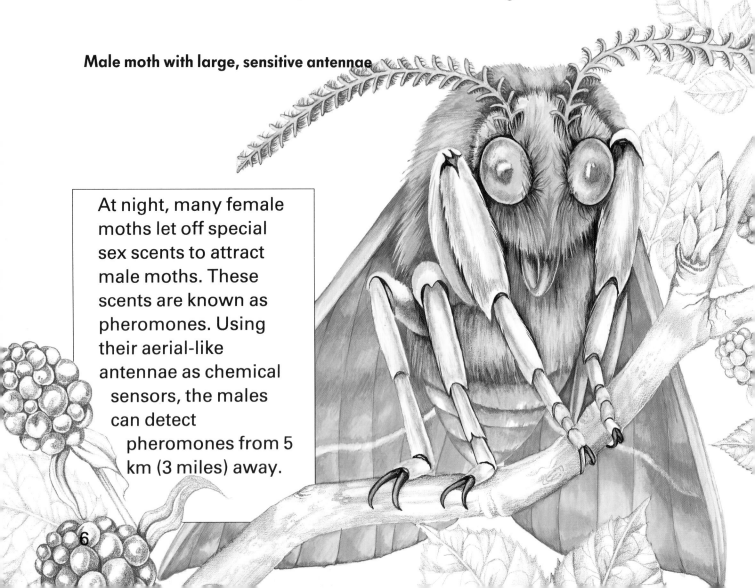

At night, many female moths let off special sex scents to attract male moths. These scents are known as pheromones. Using their aerial-like antennae as chemical sensors, the males can detect pheromones from 5 km (3 miles) away.

Nightjars are night-time predators. They use a system called "echolocation" to find their prey. The bird emits sounds as it is flying along. These sounds strike an insect and bounce back. The nightjar listens for the echoes, which allow it to determine the insect's position accurately.

A nightjar homes in on a moth

Aerial hunters

Owls live in woods and forests. They rest in trees during the day. But as darkness falls they take to the air and begin to hunt. Owls feed on mice, voles and small birds. Sitting on a perch, a Barn Owl will listen for the slightest squeak or rustle from the ground below. To do this it moves its head from side to side, up and down, and even right around. When it detects an animal the owl flies towards it, using its sharp vision to home in on its target. Owls' eyes are up to a hundred times more sensitive to light than ours, and they have the widest field of vision of any bird.

Nightjars and nighthawks hunt insects at night. They open their enormous mouths as they fly and gobble up mosquitoes and moths in their path. Some will even snap up other birds if they come across them.

A Barn Owl swooping in for the kill ▷

Scavengers and predators

Many predators – animals that kill and eat other animals – hunt at night. Civets, genets and mongooses, for example, are nocturnal predators. The animals they hunt, their prey, include birds, mice and insects. Leopards and tigers stalk their antelope prey in the darkness. Hyenas are efficient night-time killers, but they are also scavengers – they feed on the leftovers of other animals' meals. A pack of hyenas will even drive a lion away from a carcass.

Wild boars mainly eat plant food, and skunks feed on insects, mice, bird and reptile eggs, and fruit. But these nocturnal animals also feed on the flesh of any dead animals that they find. If a skunk is disturbed while eating, it stands on its front paws and squirts a jet of foul-smelling liquid at the intruder. It will aim for the eyes. The liquid causes temporary blindness.

Spotted Hyenas try to bring down a young Zebra

10

A tiger moves its kill to a safe place ▷

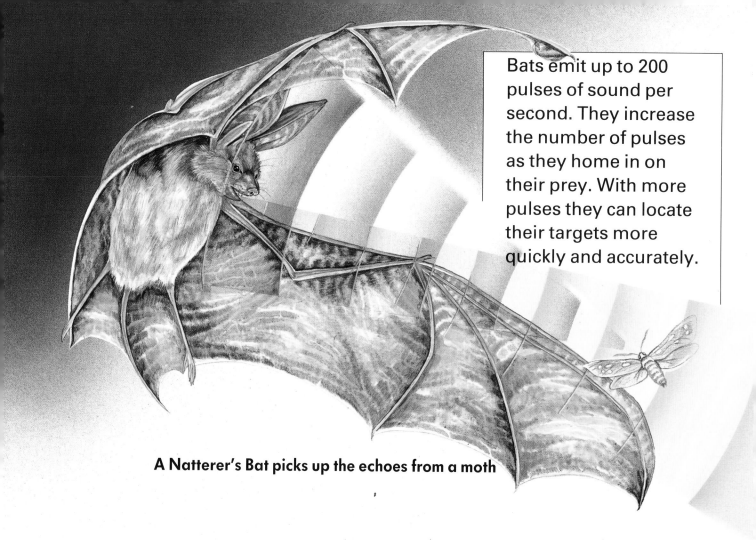

Bats emit up to 200 pulses of sound per second. They increase the number of pulses as they home in on their prey. With more pulses they can locate their targets more quickly and accurately.

A Natterer's Bat picks up the echoes from a moth

Bats

Bats spend the daytime sleeping in caves, trees or old buildings. They sleep hanging upside-down, sometimes in huge groups of a million or more. They start to search for food soon after the sun has set. Most bats feed on insects, which they capture while in flight. They have small eyes and poor vision – hence the saying "as blind as a bat".

Like nightjars, bats use echolocation to pin-point insects in the air. Horseshoe Bats, for example, have flaps of skin on the nose. They use these to direct sounds which they fire out of their nostrils. They send out many pulses of sound each second and listen for any echoes. Bats have very good hearing. Their large, curved ears collect sounds from over a wide area. Bats that live in caves also use echolocation to find their way around in dark, cramped spaces.

Brown Bats use echolocation when flying ▷

Avoiding the heat

Snakes, lizards and all other reptiles are "cold-blooded". Their body temperature depends on their surroundings. Many reptiles that live in deserts are nocturnal. They avoid the heat and bright light of the day by burrowing or sleeping in the shade, and come out when darkness falls. Pit vipers like the rattlesnake, for example, rely on heat from sun-warmed rocks and soil. They hunt nocturnal mice, frogs, lizards and sleeping birds at night.

Many desert mammals burrow in the ground to escape the fierce heat. They include jerboas, gerbils and some rats and mice. Desert jerboas feed on insects and plants. They have large eyes, giving them good night vision, and their big ears can detect the faintest of sounds. They feed on insects and plants and often carry food back to their burrows to eat in safety or store until later.

These desert animals all escape the midday sun by digging burrows in the ground

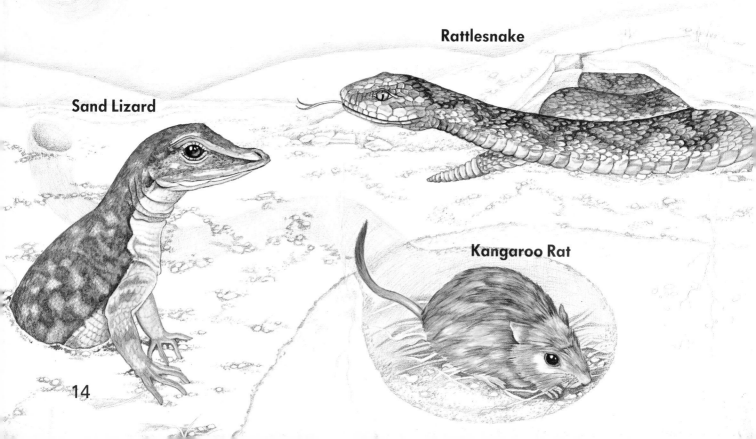

Rattlesnake

Sand Lizard

Kangaroo Rat

Spiders and scorpions

As night falls a Trapdoor Spider will gently raise the silken door at the entrance to its burrow. Any insect that comes too near is seized by a lightning swoop of the spider's front legs. The prey is then dragged into the burrow and eaten. Bird-eating Spiders are also night-time hunters. They are covered in hairs that are highly sensitive to vibrations. Occasionally they catch birds, but usually they prey on frogs, insects and other spiders. They can give a person a very painful bite.

Scorpions hunt spiders, centipedes and insects at night. They wait in their lairs for their victims to pass by. Then they strike. They catch their prey with their pincer-like claws, and paralyse or kill it using the sting at the end of their tail. During the day scorpions live in hollows beneath rocks or in burrows up to 1m (3 ft) deep.

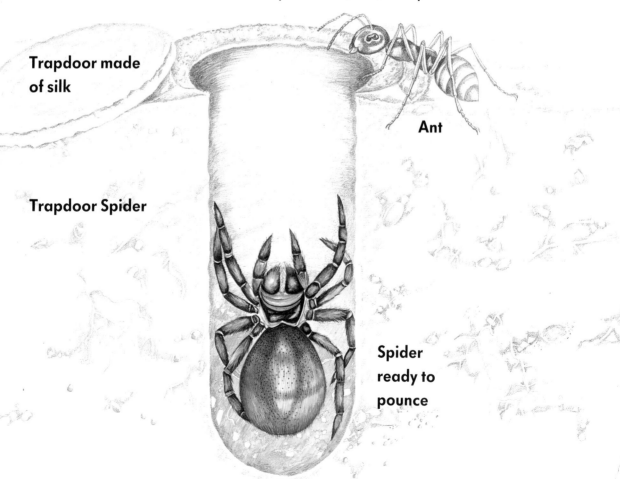

Trapdoor made of silk

Ant

Trapdoor Spider

Spider ready to pounce

This grasshopper strayed too close to a scorpion's den ▷

Tarsiers are only the size of squirrels. But they can leap 2m (6.5 ft) from branch to branch in utter darkness. They almost never fall.

In bright light, a tarsier's pupils will close up, as here

Primates

Tree-shrews, lorises, pottos and tarsiers closely resemble our distant ancestors. Together with monkeys, apes and humans, they form a group of mammals known as primates. And like the early primates, most of them are small tree-living animals that are active at night. They spend the day sleeping, either inside a hollow tree or clinging to a branch with their hands and feet. They eat fruit, leaves, insects and even frogs.

Tarsiers and lorises have large, forward-facing eyes. These help the animals to judge distances accurately as they move from tree to tree in the starlit forests. Their hearing is also good. Like bats, they have large ears. They move these constantly to locate the sources of sounds. Slow Lorises spend their entire lives in trees. Females make an eerie whistle at night. This is believed to be a mating call used to attract male Slow Lorises.

Slow Lorises live in the rain forests of southern Asia ▷

Urban visitors

Many animals of the night make their homes close to human settlements. Parks and gardens provide refuge for snails, slugs and earthworms. These creatures live in damp, shady places among the leaf litter or in the soil. They emerge at night or on wet days and go searching for plant food and decaying material. Because they move slowly and have few defences, many are eaten by Badgers and Hedgehogs. These nocturnal predators use their keen senses of smell and hearing to find their prey.

Raccoons and Red Foxes also eat earthworms. But they prefer to prey on mice, frogs, fish, and birds. In parts of North America and Europe they are thought of as pests. They raid rubbish bins and have been known to kill cats, chickens and even lambs.

A North American (above) and two European night-time garden visitors

Raccoon

Hedgehog

Garden Snail

In a split-second, a frog can shoot out its long and sticky tongue, catch an insect in flight, and pull the prey into its mouth.

Frogs and toads

Spring is the mating season for frogs and toads in the temperate parts of the world. The night air is filled with their croaks, chirps and grunts. All frogs and toads are more active at night. This is because they are safer from attack by reptiles and birds, most of which hunt in the day. There is also little danger of their moist skin drying out at night, and there are plenty of insects to eat.

Frogs and toads mainly rely on vision to catch their food. Even in very dim light, the slightest movement of a small animal will draw their attention. Their eyes bulge out from the head, giving them a clear, all-round view of food or approaching danger.

Male frogs croak to tell females where to find them ▷

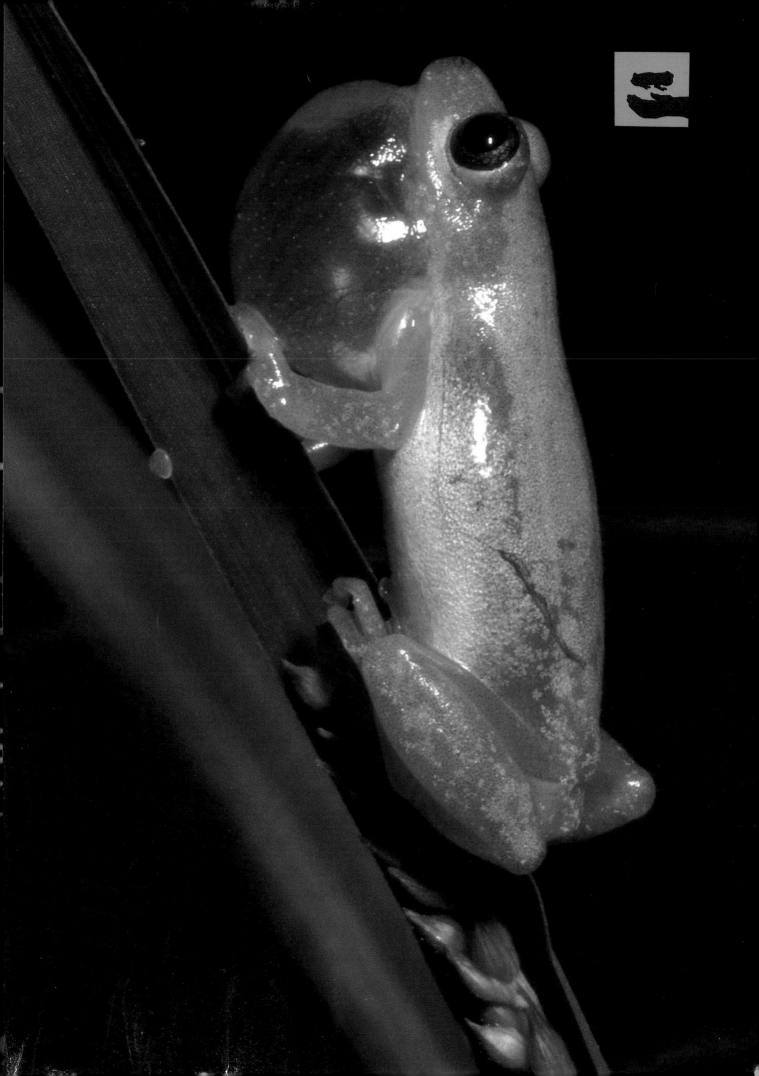

Insect eaters

"Aardvark" means "earth pig". It is an appropriate name, for this noctural grassland animal is about the size of a large pig. It uses its long mobile snout to root around in the earth for food. The Aardvark mostly feeds on ants and termites. Its sense of hearing is very good: it can detect a column of ants on the move from the rustling noise made by the insects.

Aardvarks are powerful animals. They rip open termite nests with their claws and lap up the insects with their long sticky tongues. Pangolins feed in the same way, but they seem to use smell rather than hearing to locate their food. When threatened, they curl up into a tight ball. Their sharp-edged scales protect them from attackers. Tree Pangolins spend most of their time high in the forest canopy, feeding from ant and termite nests.

Tree Pangolins are almost blind, but have strong senses of smell and hearing

An Aardvark sleeps after its night-time feast of termites ▷

Pouched animals

Animals like kangaroos and the Koala are mammals, as we are. But unlike us, they give birth to tiny young that develop in a pouch outside their mother's belly. Animals that do this are known as marsupials. Most marsupials are plant-eaters and many are nocturnal.

Possums move through forests under cover of darkness, travelling between feeding and resting sites. They have good senses of hearing and smell. Possums mark their areas with their urine and dung, and rub one another with scents from skin glands. Marsupial meat-eaters, such as the Tasmanian Devil and Australian Native Cat, have good sight, hearing and smell. They are excellent hunters. They prey on birds, lizards, insects, rats and rabbits. Some are also scavengers.

A Tasmanian Devil shows its teeth

This Virginian Opossum is carrying her young on her back ▷

Survival file

Animals of the night are many and varied. Some, like the primates and several opossums, are threatened with extinction. This may be through destruction of their forest homes for timber and to create new farmland. Or it may be a result of hunting by local people for their skins and meat. Other nocturnal animals, such as the Common Raccoon, are thought of as pests. They often venture into towns and cause chaos by raiding rubbish tips and attacking pets. But as with all nocturnal animals, because they are most active when it is dark, we know little about their behaviour. This makes it more difficult to manage and protect them.

Kangaroos slaughtered for their meat

Nocturnal creatures such as tigers and leopards are now the subject of international conservation agreements. For centuries, these animals were killed for "sport" or to provide fur coats or rugs. Fifty years ago there were still about 30,000 Indian Tigers remaining. Today there are less than 3,000, although numbers have been increasing since the start of the Save the Tiger Campaign in the 1970s, and the creation of reserves.

Owls need barns like this one to roost in

A Leopard skin for sale

Sometimes nocturnal (and daytime) creatures are threatened because of harmful diseases. The European Badger, for example, may carry the disease tuberculosis. Farmers then kill sick badgers to stop the infection from spreading to cattle. In North America the Common Raccoon may carry another disease, rabies, which can be fatal to pets – and to people. An infected animal must be killed if the spread of the disease is to be prevented.

Kangaroos and wallabies, many of which are nocturnal, are often killed deliberately to keep their numbers under control. These animals are regarded as pests because they eat grass needed for sheep and goats. Many species of bats and owls have suffered from our increasing use of pesticides, and from the removal of farm buildings in which they roost and nest.

A Red Fox on a raid

Identification chart

This chart shows you a variety of large and small animals of the night. There are mammals, birds, reptiles, amphibians and invertebrates from different regions of the world. Notice how the larger animals all have well-developed sense organs – large eyes, a long snout with touch-sensitive whiskers, or large ears. These help the animals to find their way, and their food, in the dark. You can see most of these animals in zoos, and a few of them in your garden.

- ○ Europe
- ○ Australia
- ○ Africa N.
- ○ N. and S. America
- ○ Madagascar
- ○ Asia

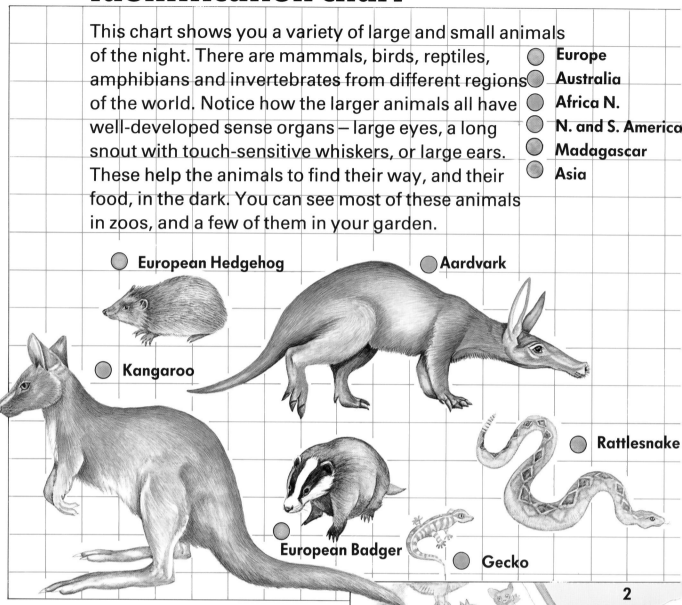

○ European Hedgehog

○ Aardvark

○ Kangaroo

○ Rattlesnake

○ European Badger

○ Gecko

2

Make a night-time animal mural

1. Using the drawings above, copy the outlines of the animals onto sheets of graph paper.

2. Tape a sheet of foil to the back of each of your outlines.

3. Cut out the animal shapes from the foil.

4. Stick the shapes onto a large sheet of black paper.

5. Hold up the large sheet in front of a torch in a dark room and make the animals glow.

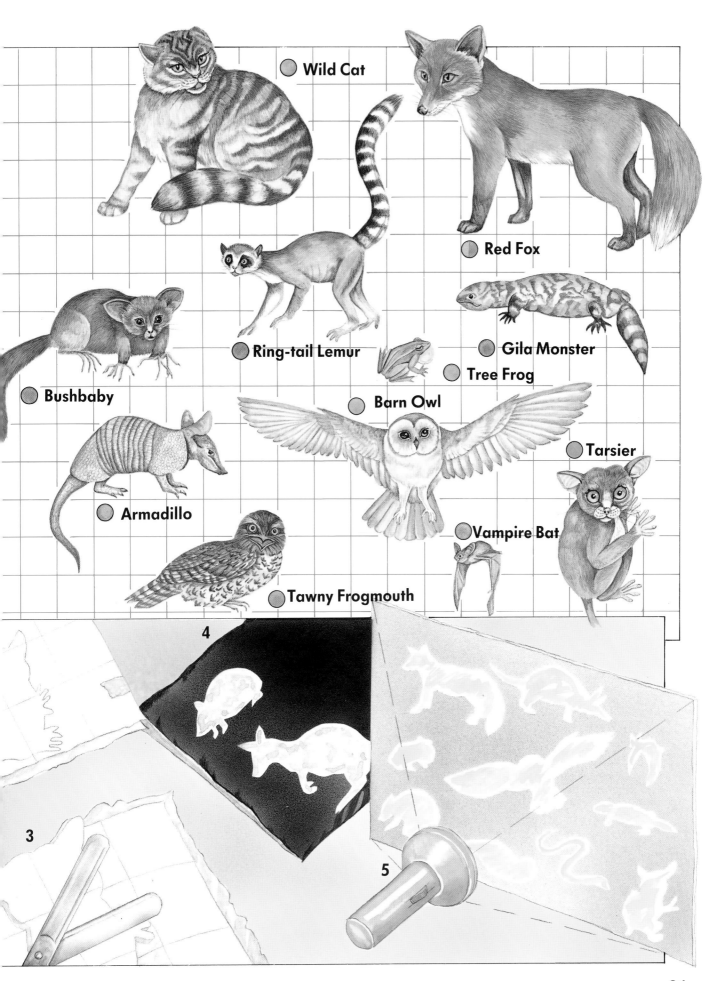

Wild Cat

Red Fox

Ring-tail Lemur

Gila Monster

Tree Frog

Bushbaby

Barn Owl

Tarsier

Armadillo

Vampire Bat

Tawny Frogmouth

4

3

5

Index

A Aardvark 24, 30
Armadillo 31

B Bat
Brown 12, 13
Horseshoe 12
Natterer's 12
bats 12, 29
burrowers 14
Bushbaby 2, 3, 31

E ears 14, 18
echolocation 8, 12
eyes 8, 12, 14, 18

F food and feeding 5,
8, 10, 12, 14, 18,
20, 22, 24
Fox
Fennec 4, 5
Red 20, 31
Frog, Tree 31
frogs 22

G gecko 14, 30
genets 10
gerbils 14
Gila Monster 31

H hearing 12, 20, 24
Hedgehog,
European 20, 30

hyenas 10

J Jerboa, Desert 14

K Kangaroo, Rat 14
Kangaroos 26, 29,
30
Koala 26

L leopards 10, 29
Loris, Slow 18
lorises 18

M marsupials 26
mating 20, 22
mice 14
mongooses 10
moths 6

N nighthawks 8, 12
nightjars 8

O opossums 26, 28,
31
Owl, Barn 8, 31
owls 8, 29

P pangolins 24
pheromones 6
possums 26
pottos 18
primates 18, 28

R Raccoon, Common
28, 29, 31
raccoons 20
Rat, Kangaroo 14
rats 14
rattlesnakes 6, 7, 14,
30

S Scorpions 16
senses 6, 20, 22, 24,
26
skunks 10
Snail, Garden 20
Spider
Bird-eating 16
Trapdoor 16

T tarsiers 18
Tasmanian Devil 26
tigers 6, 7, 10, 29
toads 22
tree-shrews 18

V Viper, Pit 14
vision 8, 22

W wallabies 29
wild boars 10
wildcat 31

Photographic Credits:
Cover, title page and pages 4, 7, 13, 15, 17, 19, 21, 23, 24, 25, 26, 27, 28 and 29 all: Bruce Coleman; pages 9 and 11: Planet Earth.